When the history of fantasy and horror fiction is being discussed, the pulp magazine *Weird Tales* is inevitably mentioned. Published on low-grade "pulp" paper, *Weird Tales* was the first newsstand magazine devoted exclusively to weird and fantastic fiction. It ran for 279 issues, from March 1923 to September 1954.

The three most important and influential writers to have their work published in the title were Rhode Island horror writer H.P. Lovecraft; the Texan creator of Conan the Cimmerian, Robert E. Howard; and the California poet, short story writer, illustrator and sculptor, Clark Ashton Smith.

"The Complete Poems from *Weird Tales*" series collects their verse in the order that it originally appeared in the pages of "The Unique Magazine".

SONG OF THE NECROMANCER & OTHERS

THE COMPLETE POEMS FROM *Weird Tales*

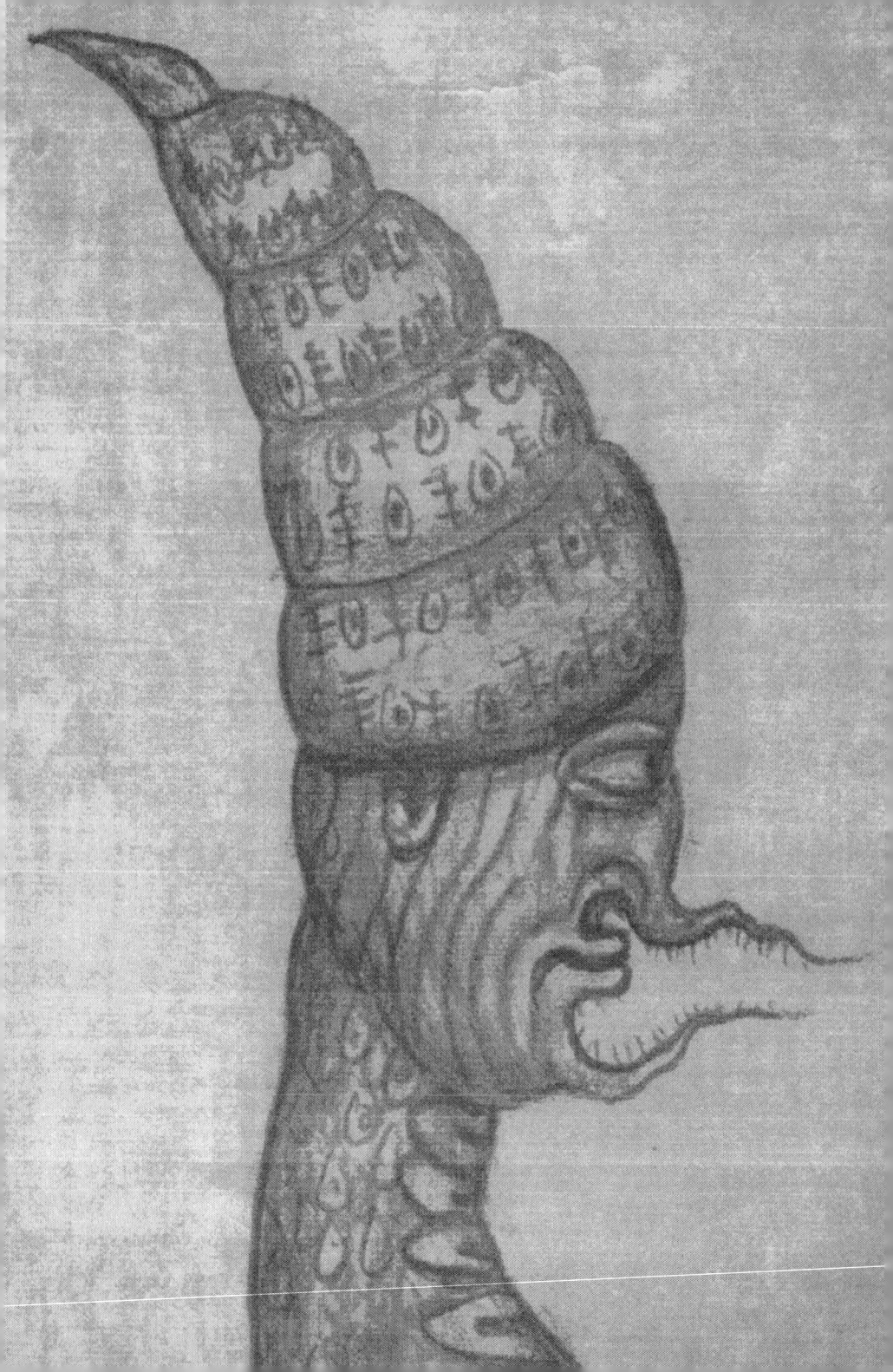

Song of the Necromancer & Others

The Complete Poems From *Weird Tales*

By Clark Ashton Smith

Compiled and with An Introduction by Stephen Jones

StanZa

SONG OF THE NECROMANCER & OTHERS
THE COMPLETE POEMS FROM *WEIRD TALES*
Copyright © CASiana Literary Enterprises, Inc. 2010
Collection and editorial material copyright © Stephen Jones 2010

COVER ART & FRONTISPIECE
Copyright © Clark Ashton Smith. Reprinted by permission of CASiana Literary Enterprises, Inc. From the collection of Stephen Jones.

ENDPAPERS
Copyright © Ann Muir Marbling 2010.

Published in March 2010 by Stanza Press, a division of PS Publishing Ltd.

The right of Clark Ashton Smith to be identified as Author of this Work has been asserted by him in accordance with the Copyright, Designs and Patents Act 1988.

This book is a work of fiction. Names, characters, places and incidents either are products of the author's imagination or are used fictitiously. Any resemblance to actual events or locales or persons, living or dead, is entirely coincidental.

ISBN
978-1-848630-80-2

Design & Layout by Michael Smith.

Printed in Great Britain by the MPG Books Group, Bodmin and King's Lynn

STANZA PRESS
GROSVENOR HOUSE
1 NEW ROAD
HORNSEA, HU18 1PG
ENGLAND

e-mail: editor@pspublishing.co.uk
Internet: www.pspublishing.co.uk

CONTENTS

x	Introduction by Stephen Jones
3	The Garden of Evil
3	The Red Moon
4	Solution
5	The Melancholy Pool
5	A Fable
6	Interrogation
7	The Saturnienne
8	Warning
8	Sonnet
10	Nyctalops
12	The Nightmare Tarn
14	*Fantaisie d'Antan*
16	Ougabalya
17	Shadows
18	Fellowship
19	In Slumber
20	Dominion
21	In Thessaly
22	Ennui
23	Song of the Necromancer
24	To Howard Phillips Lovecraft

26	Outlanders
27	Farewell to Eros
28	The Prophet Speaks
30	Bacchante
31	The Phoenix
32	Witch Dance
34	Necromancy
34	Dialogue
35	Desert Dweller
36	The Sorcerer to His Love
37	Resurrection
38	To the Chimera
39	Do You Forget, Enchantress?
40	Luna Aeternalia
42	"Not Altogether Sleep"
42	Sonnet for the Psychoanalysts
43	"O Golden-Tongued Romance"
45	Don Quixote on Market Street

ACKNOWLEDGEMENTS

Special thanks to Peter and Nicky Crowther, Mike Smith, April Derleth, Joshua Bilmes, John Berlyne, David E. Schultz, S.T. Joshi, CASiana Literary Enterprises and Arkham House Publishers, Inc. for their help compiling this volume. The poems collected in this volume are the "classic texts" as they originally appeared in *Weird Tales, Dark of the Moon: Poems of Fantasy and the Macbre, The Dark Chateau and Other Poems, Selected Poems* and other publications.

'Introduction' copyright © Stephen Jones 2010.
'The Garden of Evil' copyright © the Popular Fiction Publishing Company. Originally published in *Weird Tales*, July-August 1923. Reprinted by permission of Arkham House Publishers, Inc.
'The Red Moon' copyright © the Popular Fiction Publishing Company. Originally published in *Weird Tales*, July-August 1923. Reprinted by permission of Arkham House Publishers, Inc.
'Solution' copyright © the Popular Fiction Publishing Company. Originally published in *Weird Tales*, January 1924. Reprinted by permission of Arkham House Publishers, Inc.
'The Melancholy Pooll' copyright © the Popular Fiction Publishing Company. Originally published in *Weird Tales*, March 1924. Reprinted by permission of Arkham House Publishers, Inc.
'A Fable' copyright © the Popular Fiction Publishing Company. Originally published in *Weird Tales*, July 1927. Reprinted by permission of Arkham House Publishers, Inc.
'Interrogation' copyright © the Popular Fiction Publishing Company. Originally published in *Weird Tales*, September 1927. Reprinted by permission of Arkham House Publishers, Inc.
'The Saturnienne' copyright © the Popular Fiction Publishing Company. Originally published in *Weird Tales*, December 1927. Reprinted by permission of Arkham House Publishers, Inc.
'Warning' copyright © the Popular Fiction Publishing Company. Originally published in *Weird Tales*, October 1928. Reprinted by permission of Arkham House Publishers, Inc.

Song of the Necromancer

'Sonnet' copyright © the Popular Fiction Publishing Company. Originally published in *Weird Tales*, April 1929. Reprinted by permission of Arkham House Publishers, Inc.
'Nyctalops' copyright © the Popular Fiction Publishing Company. Originally published in *Weird Tales*, October 1929. Reprinted by permission of Arkham House Publishers, Inc.
'The Nightmare Tarn' copyright © the Popular Fiction Publishing Company. Originally published in *Weird Tales*, November 1929. Reprinted by permission of Arkham House Publishers, Inc.
'Fantaisie d'Antan' copyright © the Popular Fiction Publishing Company. Originally published in *Weird Tales*, December 1929. Reprinted by permission of Arkham House Publishers, Inc.
'Ougabalya' copyright © the Popular Fiction Publishing Company. Originally published in *Weird Tales*, January 1930. Reprinted by permission of Arkham House Publishers, Inc.
'Shadows' copyright © the Popular Fiction Publishing Company. Originally published in *Weird Tales*, February 1930. Reprinted by permission of Arkham House Publishers, Inc.
'Fellowship' copyright © the Popular Fiction Publishing Company. Originally published in *Weird Tales*, October 1930. Reprinted by permission of Arkham House Publishers, Inc.
'In Slumber' copyright © the Popular Fiction Publishing Company. Originally published in *Weird Tales*, August 1934. Reprinted by permission of Arkham House Publishers, Inc.
'Dominion' copyright © the Popular Fiction Publishing Company. Originally published in *Weird Tales*, June 1935. Reprinted by permission of Arkham House Publishers, Inc.
'In Thessaly' copyright © the Popular Fiction Publishing Company. Originally published in *Weird Tales*, November 1935. Reprinted by permission of Arkham House Publishers, Inc.
'Ennui' originally published in *The Smart Set*, September 1918; reprinted in *Weird Tales*, May 1936. Reprinted by permission of Arkham House Publishers, Inc.
'Song of the Necromancer' copyright © the Popular Fiction Publishing Company. Originally published in *Weird Tales*, February 1937. Reprinted by permission of Arkham House Publishers, Inc.

Clark Ashton Smith [signature]

'To Howard Phillips Lovecraft' copyright © the Popular Fiction Publishing Company. Originally published in *Weird Tales*, July 1937. Reprinted by permission of Arkham House Publishers, Inc.
'Outlanders' copyright © the Popular Fiction Publishing Company. Originally published in *Weird Tales*, June 1938. Reprinted by permission of Arkham House Publishers, Inc.
'Farewell to Eros' copyright © the Popular Fiction Publishing Company. Originally published in *Weird Tales*, June 1938. Reprinted by permission of Arkham House Publishers, Inc.
'The Prophet Speaks' copyright © the Popular Fiction Publishing Company. Originally published in *Weird Tales*, September 1938. Reprinted by permission of Arkham House Publishers, Inc.
'Bacchante' copyright © *Weird Tales*. Originally published in *Weird Tales*, December 1939. Reprinted by permission of Arkham House Publishers, Inc.
'The Phoenix' copyright © *Weird Tales*. Originally published in *Weird Tales*, May 1940. Reprinted by permission of Arkham House Publishers, Inc.
'Witch-Dance' copyright © *Weird Tales*. Originally published in *Weird Tales*, September 1941. Reprinted by permission of Arkham House Publishers, Inc.
'Necromancy' copyright © *Weird Tales*. Originally published in *Weird Tales*, March 1943. Reprinted by permission of Arkham House Publishers, Inc.
'Dialogue' copyright © *Weird Tales*. Originally published (as by Timeus Gaylord) in *Weird Tales*, May 1943. Reprinted by permission of Arkham House Publishers, Inc.
'Desert Dweller' copyright © *Weird Tales*. Originally published in *Weird Tales*, July 1943. Reprinted by permission of Arkham House Publishers, Inc.
'The Sorcerer to His Love' copyright © *Weird Tales*. Originally published in *Weird Tales*, September 1945. Reprinted by permission of Arkham House Publishers, Inc.
'Resurrection' copyright © *Weird Tales*. Originally published in *Weird Tales*, July 1947. Reprinted by permission of Arkham House Publishers, Inc.

Song of the Necromancer

'To the Chimera' originally published in *The Auburn Journal*, April 3, 1924; reprinted in *Weird Tales*, September 1948. Reprinted by permission of Arkham House Publishers, Inc.
'Do You Forget, Enchantress?' copyright © *Weird Tales*. Originally published in *Weird Tales*, March 1950. Reprinted by permission of Arkham House Publishers, Inc.
'Luna Aeternalis' copyright © *Weird Tales*. Originally published in *Weird Tales*, May 1950. Reprinted by permission of Arkham House Publishers, Inc.
'"Not Altogether Sleep"' copyright © Clark Ashton Smith 1951. Originally published in *The Dark Chateau and Other Poems*; reprinted (as 'Not Altogether Sleep') in *Weird Tales*, January 1952. Reprinted by permission of Arkham House Publishers, Inc.
'Sonnet for the Psychoanalyste' copyright © Clark Ashton Smith 1951. Originally published in *The Dark Chateau and Other Poems*; reprinted in *Weird Tales*, January 1952. Reprinted by permission of Arkham House Publishers, Inc.
'"O Golden-Tongued Romance"' copyright © Clark Ashton Smith 1951. Originally published in The Dark Chateau and Other Poems; reprinted (as 'O Golden-Tongued Romance') in *Weird Tales*, March 1952. Reprinted by permission of Arkham House Publishers, Inc.
'Don Quixote on Market Street' copyright © Clark Ashton Smith 1951. Originally published in *The Dark Chateau and Other Poems*; reprinted in *Weird Tales*, March 1953. Reprinted by permission of Arkham House Publishers, Inc.

INTRODUCTION

CLARK ASHTON SMITH (1893-1961) was a poet, short story writer, illustrator and sculptor.

One of the "big three" authors to appear in the legendary pulp magazine *Weird Tales*—alongside H.P. Lovecraft and Robert E. Howard—his fiction and artwork was published in a wide variety of magazines, anthologies and collections.

For most of his sixty-eight years, Smith lived in a small cabin in the woods near Auburn, California, and during his lifetime he published nearly twice as many books of poetry than he did short stories.

As a child, Smith was almost entirely self-educated after illness cut short his formal learning. Inspired by the works of Edgar Allan Poe and with a youthful appreciation of the Arabian Nights, he began writing at the age of eleven and had sold four short stories to magazines by the age of seventeen.

During this period, Smith's major literary influence was the Romantic poetry of San Francisco bohemian and newspaper columnist George Sterling. A protégé of Ambrose Bierce and a close friend of the novelist Jack London, Sterling worked in the tradition of Keats and Shelley.

Although that baroque style of florid verse had passed mostly out of vogue by the early part of the twentieth century, it remained popular in California into the early 1920s thanks to a remarkable group of poets now known as the California Romantics.

Smith was heavily influenced by Sterling's infamous 1907 poem 'A Wine of Wizardry', and it was the young writer's own gift for verse that eventually brought him to the attention of the more experienced poet in 1911.

Smith's first collection of poetry, *The Star-Treader and Other Poems* (1912), was issued by Sterling's own publisher, A.M. Robertson, in an estimated first edition of 2,000 copies. The slim volume was immediately hailed as the work of a prodigy and the

Song of the Necromancer

young poet's fame even spread across the Atlantic where, in a 1916 edition of the London *Evening News*, the Welsh fantasist Arthur Machen reviewed the book and observed that the author, "shows in many of his verses a great admiration for 'the grand manner'; he builds his poems up as if they were cathedrals".

Although Smith did not make much money from his first book, he went on to produce two further volumes of poetry, *Odes and Sonnets* (1918) and the self-published *Ebony and Crystal: Poems in Verse and Prose* (1922), the latter containing his epic verse, 'The Hashish-Eater; or, The Apocalypse of Evil', written at the age of twenty-seven in just ten days.

However, despite having achieved significant acclaim, Smith received little financial reward for his poetry and he survived on odd jobs and a number of small stipends.

It was the visionary quality of Smith's poetry that brought him to the attention of fledgling author H.P. Lovecraft, who declared that, "The magnificence of 'The Hashish-Eater' is beyond description".

The two began corresponding in 1922, and Lovecraft soon encouraged his new friend to send his visions of cosmic fantasy and horror to the Chicago-based pulp magazine *Weird Tales*.

The following year, two of Smith's poems, 'The Garden of Evil' and 'The Red Moon', appeared in the July-August edition, and over the next three decades the author was represented in "The Unique Magazine" with thirty-nine poems and more than sixty stories.

One of his poems, 'Dialogue', appeared in the May 1943 issue under the pseudonym "Timeus Gaylord"—a combination of Smith's English-born father's first name and his mother's family name.

With a poet's grasp of language and tone, the author had command of a comprehensive vocabulary which he obtained as a child by studying and learning an unabridged dictionary from A to Z, and then each word's derivations from other languages.

In a 1950 letter to S.J. Sackett he explained: "As to my employment of an ornate style, using many words of classic origin and exotic colour, I can only say that it is designed to produce effects of language and rhythm which could not possibly be achieved by a vocabulary restricted to what is known as 'basic English'".

Much of Smith's writings were inspired by the French Decadence movement, and he taught himself to read and write in both French and Spanish just so that he could read and translate his favourite poets in those languages. His translations of eight poems by Charles Pierre Baudelaire (one under the "Gaylord" alias) and another by Paul Verlaine eventually found their way into the pages of *Weird Tales*.

"Speaking as a reader," Smith wrote in the magazine's letters column, 'The Eyrie', in the December 1930 edition, "I should like to say that *Weird Tales* is the one magazine that gives its writers ample imaginative freeway."

After Smith's poem 'Dominion' appeared in the June 1935 issue, fellow *Weird Tales* contributor Robert E. Howard wrote: "I am not exaggerating when I say that I do not consider that I ever read a finer poem than that. I'd give my trigger-finger for the ability to make words flame and burn as you do".

Less than a year later Howard was dead by his own hand, and Lovecraft died of cancer in 1937. Smith's poem 'To Howard Phillips Lovecraft' appeared in the July 1937 issue of *Weird Tales* as a tribute.

Another *Weird Tales* writer and Lovecraft correspondent, Donald Wandrei, had helped finance Smith's fourth volume of poetry, *Sandalwood* (1925), and in late 1935 Smith began compiling a new collection of poems to be published by Lovecraft's "boy protégé" Robert H. Barlow under the title *Incantations*.

When Barlow's plans were delayed, Smith's collection of ten poems entitled *Nero and Other Poems* appeared in May 1937 from Clyde Beck's The Futile Press in a printing of 150 copies. A month after publication, Beck had a further Smith poem and an essay by David Warren Ryder printed up on separate sheets and laid them into the remaining editions.

Song of the Necromancer

Around the same time the author submitted a selection of his poems to a British publisher, but nothing came of it.

Smith had developed an alcohol problem and, following Lovecraft's death, his own health deteriorated. Forced to live on a meagre budget, he was reduced to taking menial jobs to survive.

Finally, in 1942, Smith's first significant volume of fiction appeared from Arkham House, the specialist publisher established by August Derleth and Donald Wandrei. Over the next few decades, the imprint brought all Smith's major fiction back into print between hardcovers, along with such poetry collections as *The Dark Chateau and Other Poems* (1951), *Spells and Philtres* (1958), *Poems in Prose* (1965) and the long-delayed *Selected Poems* (1971).

After entering into a late-life marriage with journalist Carolyn Jones Dorman in 1954, Smith experienced another burst of creative energy during the middle-to-late 1950s, when he produced his final batch of new short fiction.

Following a series of minor strokes, Clark Ashton Smith died peacefully in his sleep in Pacific Grove on August 14, 1961. He left behind a unique legacy of fantasy fiction and poetry which is as imaginative and decadent today as when it was first published in the pulp magazines more than eighty years ago.

In a letter to August Derleth written in August 1961, Frank Belknap Long, another of the "Lovecraft Circle", described Smith as, "a very fine poet who never received the recognition he deserved and whose entire life was, in the main, ill-starred, made somber by the frustration which one could sense in almost everything he wrote".

—Stephen Jones
London, England
September 2009

SONG OF THE NECROMANCER & OTHERS

THE COMPLETE POEMS FROM *Weird Tales*

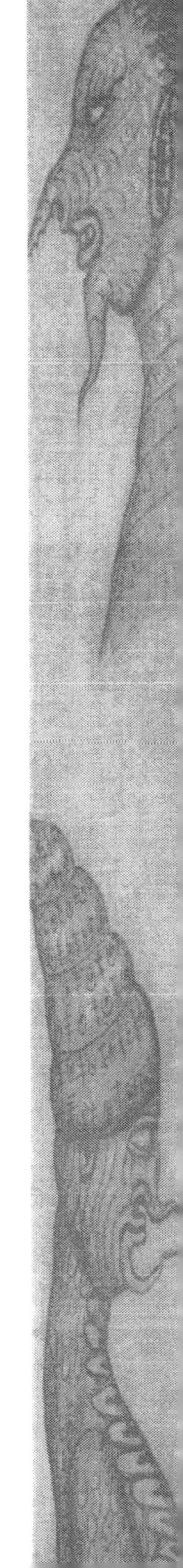

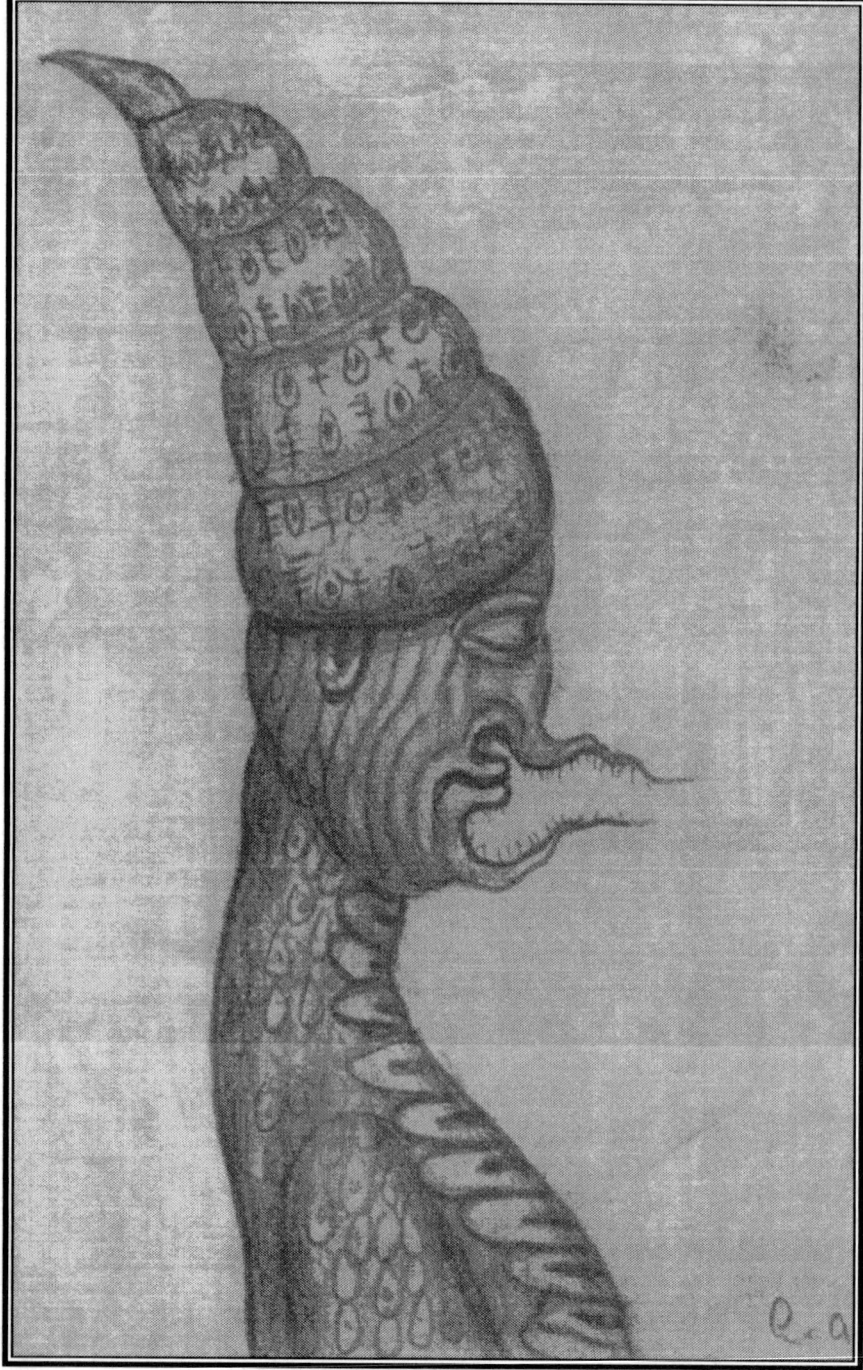

THE GARDEN OF EVIL

Thy soul is like a secret garden-close,
Where roots of cleft mandragoras enwreathe;
Where bergamot and fumitory breathe,
And ivy winds its flower with the rose.

The lolling weeds of Lethe, green or wan,
Exhale their fatal languors on the light;
From out infernal grails of aconite
Poisons and dews are proffered to the dawn.

Here, when the moon's phantasmal fingers grope
To find the marbles of a hidden tomb,
There sings the cypress-perchèd nightingale;

And all the silver-bellied serpents pale
Their ruby eyes amid the blossoms ope,
To lift and listen in the ghostly gloom.

THE RED MOON

The hills, a-throng with swarthy pine,
Press up the pale and hollow sky,
And the squat cypresses on high
Reach from the lit horizon-line.

They reach, they reach, with gnarlèd hands—
Malignant hags, obscene and dark—
While the red moon, a demons' ark,
Is borne along the mystic lands.

Song of the Necromancer

SOLUTION

The ghostly fire that walks the fen,
Tonight thine only light shall be;
On lethal ways thy soul shall pass,
And prove the stealthy, coiled morass
With mocking mists for company.

On roads thou goest not again,
To shores where thou hast never gone,
Fare onward, though the shuddering queach
And serpent-rippled waters reach
Like seepage-pools of Acheron

Beside thee; and the twisted reeds,
Close-raddled as a witch's net,
Enwind thy knees, and cling and clutch
Like wreathing adders; though the touch
Of the blind air be dank and wet

As from a wounded Thing that bleeds
In cloud and darkness overhead—
Fare onward, where thy dreams of yore
In splendor drape the fetid shore
And pestilential waters dead.

And though the toads' irrison rise
Like grinding of Satanic racks,
And spectral willows, gaunt and grey,
Gibber along thy shrouded way,
Where vipers lie with livid backs

And watch thee with their sulphurous eyes—
Fare onward, till thy feet shall slip
Deep in the sudden pool ordained,
And all the noisome draught be drained
That turns to Lethe on the lip.

The Melancholy Pool

Marked by that priesthood of the Night's misrule,
The shadow-cowled, imprecatory trees—
Cypress that guarded woodland secrecies
And graves that waited for delaying ghoul,
Nathless I neared the melancholy pool,
Chief care of all, but closelier sentinelled
By those whose roots were deepest in dead eld.
Where the thwart-woven boughs were wet and cool
As with a mist of poison, I drew near
To mark the tired stars peer dimly down
Through riven branches from the height of space,
And shudder in those waters with quick fear,
Where in black deeps the pale moon seemed to drown—
A haggard girl, with dead, despairing face.

A Fable

O lords and gods that are! the assigning tide, upon
Some prowless beach where a forgotten fisher dwells,
At last will leave the sea-flung jars of Solomon;

And he, the fisher, fumbling 'mid the weeds and shells,
Shall find them, and shall rive the rusted seals, and free
The djinns that shall tread down thy towering iron hells

And turn to homeless rack thy walled Reality;
That shall remould thy monuments and mountains flown,
And lift Atlantis on their shoulders from the sea

To flaunt her kraken-fouled necropoles unknown;
And raise from realm-deep ice the boreal cities pale
With towers that man has neither built nor
 overthrown...

O lords and gods that are! I tell a future tale.

Song of the Necromancer

INTERROGATION

Love, will you look with me
Upon the phosphor-litten labor of the worm—
Time's minister, who toils for his appointed term,
And has for fee
All superannuate loves, and all the loves to be?

Love, can you see, as I,
The corpses, ghosts and demons mingled with the
   crowd?
The djinns that men have freed, grown turbulent and
   proud?
Alastor, Asmodai?
And all-unheeded envoys from the stars on high?

Know you the gulfs below,
Where darkling Erebus on Erebus is driven
Between the molecules—atom from atom riven,
And tossing to and fro,
Incessant, like the souls on Dante's wind of woe?

Know you the deeps above?
The terror and vertigo of those who gaze too long
Upon the crystal skies unclouded? Are you strong
With me to prove
Even in thought or dream the dreadful pits above?

Know you the gulfs within?
The larvae, the minotaurs of labyrinths undared?
The somber foam of seas by cryptic sirens shared?
The pestilence and sin
Borne by the flapping shroud of liches met within?

The Saturnienne

Beneath the skies of Saturn, pale and many-mooned,
Her palace is;
Her wyvern-warded spires of celadon, enruned
With names benign and mightier names of malefice,
Illume with saffron phares
A marish by the black, lethargic seas lagooned;
Her dragon-holden stairs
Go down in coiling jet and gold on some unplumbed
   abyss.

Long as a leaping flame, exalted over all,
Across the sun
Her banners bear Aidennic blooms armorial
And beasts infernal on a field of ciclaton;
Amid her agate courts,
Like to a demon ichor, towering proud and tall,
A scarlet fountain spurts,
To fall upon parterres of dwale and deathly hebenon.

From out her amber windows, gazing languidly
On a weird land
Where conium and cannabis and upas-tree
Seem wrought in verdigris against the copper sand,
She sees and sees again
A trailing salt like leprous dragons from the sea
Far-crawled upon the fen;
And foam of monster-cloven gulfs beyond a fallow
   strand.

Or, looking from her turrets to the south and north,
She notes the gleam
Of molied mountains and of rivers pouring forth,
Clear as the dawn, to fail in fulvous rill and stream

Song of the Necromancer

The widening waste amid;
Or swell the fallen meres, abominable, swarth,
In green mirages hid,
To be the unquested grails of hell, of death and deathful
  dream.

Warning

Hast heard the voices of the fen,
That softly sing a lethal rune
Where reeds have caught the fallen moon—
A song more sweet than conium is,
Or honey-blended cannabis,
To draw the dreaming feet of men
On ways where none goes forth again?

Beneath the closely woven grass,
The coiling syrt, more soft and deep
Than some divan where lovers sleep,
Is fain of all who wander there;
And arms that glimmer, vague and bare,
Beckon within the lone morass
Where only dead things dwell and pass.

Beware! the voices float and fall
Half-heard, and haply sweet to thee
As are the runes of memory
And murmurs of a voice foreknown
In days when love dwelt not alone:
Beware! for where the voices call,
Slow waters weave thy charnel pall.

Sonnet

Empress with eyes more sad and aureate
Than sunset ebbing on a summer coast,
What gold chimera lovest thou the most—
What gryphon with emblazoned wings elate,
Or dragon straying from the dim estate
Of kings that sway the continents uttermost
Of old Saturnus? Or what god, or ghost,
Or spacial demon for thy spirit's mate
Art fain to choose? Howbeit, in thy heart,
Though void as now to vision and desire
The days and years deny thee, shall abide
The passion of the impossible, the pride
Of lust immortal for the monstrous ire
And pain of love in scarlet worlds apart.

Song of the Necromancer

NYCTALOPS

Ye that see in darkness
When the moon is drowned
In the coiling fen-mist
Far along the ground—
Ye that see in darkness,
Say, what have ye found?

—We have seen strange atoms
Trysting on the air—
The dust of vanished lovers
Long parted in despair,
And dust of flowers that withered
In worlds of otherwhere.

We have seen the nightmares
Winging down the sky,
Bat-like and silent,
To where the sleepers lie;
We have seen the bosoms
Of the succubi.

We have seen the crystal
Of dead Medusa's tears.
We have watched the undines
That wane in stagnant weirs,
And mandrakes madly dancing
By black, blood-swollen meres.

We have seen the satyrs
Their ancient loves renew
With moon-white nymphs of cypress,
Pale dryads of the yew,
In the tall grass of graveyards
Weighed down with evening's dew.

We have seen the darkness
Where charnel things decay,
Where atom moves with atom
In shining swift array,
Like ordered constellations
On some sidereal way.

We have seen fair colors
That dwell not in the light—
Intenser gold and iris
Occult and recondite;
We have seen the black suns
Pouring forth the night.

Song of the Necromancer

THE NIGHTMARE TARN

I sat beside the moonless tarn alone,
In darkness where a mumbling air was blown—
A moulded air, insufferably fraught
With dust of plundered charnels: there was naught
In this my dream but darkness and the wind,
The blowing dust, the stagnant waters blind,
And sombre boughs of pine or cypress old
Wherefrom a rain of ashes dark and cold
At whiles fell on me, or was driven by
To feed the tongueless tarn; within the sky
The stars were like a failing phosphor wan
In gutted tombs from which the worms have gone.
But though the dust and ashes in one cloud
Blinded and stifled me as might a shroud,
And though the foul putrescent waters gave
Upon my face the fetors of the grave,
Though all was black corruption and despair,
I could not stir, like mandrake rooted there,
And with mine every breath I seemed to raise
The burden of some charnel of old days,
Where, tier on tier, the leaden coffins lie.

While sluggish black eternities went by
I waited; on the darkness of my dream
There fell nor lantern-flame nor lightning-gleam,
Nor gleam of moon or meteor; the wind
Withdrawn as in some sighing tomb, declined,
And all the dust was fallen; the waters drear
Lay still as blood of corpses. Loud and near
The cry of one who drowned in her despair
Came to me from the filthy tarn; the air
Shuddered thereat, and all my heart was grown
A place of fears the nether hell might own,
And prey to monstrous wings and beaks malign:

Clark Ashton Smith

For, lo! the voice, O dearest love, was thine!
And I—I could not stir: the dreadful weight
Of tomb on ancient tomb accumulate
Lay on my limbs and stifled all my breath,
And when I strove to cry, the dust of death
Had filled my mouth, nor any whisper came
To answer thee, who called upon my name!

Song of the Necromancer

FANTAISIE D'ANTAN

Lost and alien lie the leas,
Purpled all with euphrasies,
Where the lunar unicorn
Breasts an amber-pouring morn
Risen from Hesperian seas
Of a main that has no bourn.
Only things impossible
There in deathless glamour dwell:
Pegasus and sagittary,
Trotting, part the ferns of faery,
Succubi and seraphim
Tryst among the cedars dim;
Where the beaded waters brim,
White limoniads arise,
Interlacing arms and tresses
With the sun-dark satyresses;
There, on Aquilonian skies,
Gryphons, questing to and fro
For the gold of long ago,
Find at eve an aureate star
In the gulf crepuscular;
There the Hyperboreans,
Pale with wisdom more than man's,
Tell the wileful centauresses
Half their holocryptic lore;
There, at noon, the tritonesses,
All bemused with mandragore,
Mate with satyrs of the shore.

Love, could we have only found
The forgotten road that runs
Under all the sunken suns
To that time-estrangèd ground,
Surely, love were proven there

More than long and lone despair;
Holden and felicitous,
Love were fortunate to us;
And we too might ever dwell,
Deathless and impossible,
In those amber-litten leas,
Circled all with euphrasies.

Song of the Necromancer

OUGABALYS

In billow-lost Poseidonis
I was the god Ougabalys:
   My three horns were of similor
Above my double diadem,
My one eye was a moon-wan gem
   Found in a monstrous meteor.

Incredible far peoples came,
Called by the thunders of my fame,
   And fleetly passed my terraced throne,
Where titan pards and lions stood,
As pours a never-lapsing flood
   Before the wind of winter blown.

Before me, many a chorister
Made offering of alien myrrh,
   And copper-bearded sailors brought,
From isles of ever-foaming seas,
Enormous lumps of ambergris
   And corals intricately wrought.

Below my glooming architraves,
One brown eternal file of slaves
   Came in from mines of chalcedon,
And camels from the long plateaux
Laid down their sard and peridoz,
   Their incense and their cinnamon.

But now, within my sunken walls,
The slow blind ocean-serpent crawls,
   And sea-worms are my ministers;
And wondering fishes pass me now,
Or press before mine eyeless brow
   As once the thronging worshippers.

Shadows

Thy shadow falls on the fount,
On the fount with the marble wall . . .
And in alien time and space
On the towns of a doomèd race
The shadows of glaciers mount;
And patchouli-shadows crawl
On the mottling of boas that bask
In the fire of a moon fantasque;
And the light shades of bamboo
Flutter and ruffle and lift,
In the silver dawn they sift
On the meadows of Xanadu . . .

They shall fall, till the light be done,
By moon and cresset and sun,
From gnomon and fir-tree and throne,
And the vine-caught monoliths leaning
In the woods of a world far-flown;
They shall pass on the dim star-dials
By the peoples of Pluto wrought;
They shall follow the shifted vials
Of a sorceress of Fomalhaut;
They shall move on the primal plains
In the broken thunder and rains;
They shall haply reel and soar
Where the red volcanoes roar
From the peaks of a blackening sun;
They shall haply float and run
From the tails of the lyre-birds preening
On the palms of a magic mead;
And their mystery none shall read,
And none shall have known their meaning
Ere night and the shadows are one.

Song of the Necromancer

FELLOWSHIP

O ye that follow the sun,
O ye that follow the light
Of the fen-fire through the night,
Are your ways in the end not one?

Ye shall know but the selfsame doom,
Ye shall sleep the selfsame sleep,
And the trench of the trooper is deep
As the vault of an emperor's tomb.

Though dolor be yours, and dearth,
And the noon be darkness above,
Or ye know delight and love
In the pleasant places of earth,

Though your mouths be mirthful or dumb,
When the worm has eaten them thin
Ye shall grin with the same white grin
At the death whereto ye are come.

In Slumber

The stench of stagnant waters broke my dream,
Wherethrough had run, with living murmur and
   gleam,
The Rivers four of the Earthly Paradise:
From the azured flame of those effulgent skies
And valleys lifting censers of vast bloom,
I was drawn down into a deathlier gloom
Than lies on Styx's fountain. By such light
As shows the newly damned their dolorous plight,
I trod the shuddering soil of that demesne
Whence larvae swarmed, malignant and obscene,
Like writhen mists from some Maremma reeking:
Through the gross air, fell incubi went seeking
Their prey that slumbered helpless; at my knee
There clung the python-bodied succubi;
I heard the wail of them that walked apart,
Each with a suckling vampire at his heart;
And, as I stumbled loathly on, the ground
Was rent with noiseless thunder all around
To pits that teemed with direr prodigies:
Grey, headless coils, and worm-shaped infamies
Unmeasured, rose above the sun that rotted
Black as a corpse in heavens thick and clotted;
The rusty clang and shaken soot of wings
Deafened and stifled me; from pestilent springs
Slime-mantled horrors boiled with fume and hiss
To plunge in frothing fury down the abyss.
Then, from an outmost circle of that hell,
The tumbling harpies came, detestable,
With beaks that in long tatters tore my breast
And wove from these their crimson, wattled nest.

Song of the Necromancer

DOMINION

Empress of all my life, it is not known to thee
What hidden world thou holdest evermore in fee;
What muffled levies rise, from mist and Lethe drawn,

Waging some goblin war at thy forgotten whim;
What travelers in lone Cimmeria, drear and dim,
Follow the rumor of thy face toward the dawn.

Plain are those nearer lands whereon thou lookest forth,
Thy fields upon the south, thy cities in the north;
But vaster is that sealed and subterraneous realm.

High towers are built for thee with hushed demonian toil
In dayless lands, and furrows drawn through a dark soil,
And sable oceans crossed by many an unstarred helm.

Though unto thee is sent a tribute of fine gold
By them that delve therefor, never shalt thou behold
How the ore is digged in mines too near to Erebus;

Though strange Sabean myrrh within thy censers fume,
Thou shalt not ever guess the Afrit-haunted gloom
Whence the rich balm was won with labor perilous.

Occulted still from thee, thy power is on lost things,
On alien seraphim that seek with desperate wings,
Flown from their dying orb, the confines of thy heaven;

Yea, still thy whisper moves, and magically stirs
To life the shapeless dust in shattered sepulchers;
And in dark bread and wine thou art the untold leaven.

But never shalt thou dream how in some far abysm
Thy lightly spoken word has been an exorcism
Driving foul spirits from a wanderer bewrayed;

With eyes fulfilled of noon, haply thou shalt not see
How, in a land illumed by suns of ebony,
Beneath thy breath the fiery shadows flame and fade.

IN THESSALY

When I lay dead in Thessaly,
The land was rife with sorcery:
Fair witches howled to Hecate,
Pouring the blood of rams by night
With many a necromantic rite
To draw me back for their delight...

But I lay dead in Thessaly
With all my lust and wizardry:
Somewhere the Golden Ass went by
To munch the rose and find again
The shape and manlihead of men:
But in my grave I stirred not then,

And the black lote in Thessaly
Its juices dripped unceasingly
Above the rotting mouth of me;
And worm and mould and graveyard must
And roots of cypress, darkly thrust,
Transformed the dead to utter dust.

Song of the Necromancer

Ennui

Thou art immured in some sad garden sown with dust
Of fruit of Sodom that bedims the summer ground,
And burdenously bows the lilies many-crowned,
Or fills the pale and ebon mouths of sleepy lust
The poppies raise. And, falling there imponderously,
Dull ashes emptied from the urns of all the dead
Have stilled the fountain and have sealed the fountain-head
And pall-wise draped the pine and flowering myrtle-tree.

Thou art becalmed upon the slothful ancient main
Where Styx and Lethe fall; where skies of stagnant grey
With the grey stagnant waters meet and merge as one:
How tardily thy torpid heart remembers pain,
And love itself, as aureate islands far away
On seas refulgent with the incredible red sun.

Song of the Necromancer

I will repeat a subtle rune—
And thronging suns of Otherwhere
Shall blaze upon the blinded air,
And spectres terrible and fair
Shall walk the riven world at noon.

The star that was mine empery
Is dust upon unwinnowed skies:
But primal dreams have made me wise,
And soon the shattered years shall rise
To my remembered sorcery.

To mantic mutterings, brief and low,
My palaces shall lift amain,
My bowers bloom; I will regain
The lips whereon my lips have lain
In rose-red twilights long ago.

Before my murmured exorcism
The world, a wispy wraith, shall flee:
A stranger earth, a weirder sea,
Peopled with shapes of Faëry,
Shall swell upon the waste abysm.

The pantheons of darkened stars
Shall file athwart the crocus dawn;
Goddess and Gorgon, Lar and faun,
Shall tread the amaranthine lawn,
And giants fight their thunderous wars.

Like graven mountains of basalt,
Dark idols of my demons there
Shall tower through bright zones of air,
Fronting the sun with level stare;
And hell shall pave my deepest vault.

Song of the Necromancer

Phantom and fiend and sorcerer
Shall serve me . . . till my term shall pass,
And I become no more, alas,
Than a frail shadow on the glass
Before some latter conjurer.

To Howard Phillips Lovecraft

Lover of hills and fields and towns antique,
How hast thou wandered hence
On ways not found before,
Beyond the dawnward spires of Providence?
Hast thou gone forth to seek
Some older bourn than these—
Some Arkham of the prime and central wizardries?
Or, with familiar felidæ,
Dost now some new and secret wood explore,
A little past the senses' farther wall—
Where spring and sunset charm the eternal path
From Earth to ether in dimensions nemoral?
Or has the Silver Key
Opened perchance for thee
Wonders and dreams and worlds ulterior?
Hast thou gone home to Ulthar or to Pnath?
Has the high king who reigns in dim Kadath
Called back his courtly, sage ambassador?
Or darkling Cthulhu sent
The Sign which makes thee now a councilor
Within that foundered fortress of the deep
Where the Old Ones stir in sleep,
Till mighty temblors shake their slumbering continent?
Lo! in this little interim of days,

Clark Ashton Smith

How far thy feet are sped
Upon the fabulous and mooted ways
Where walk the mythic dead!
For us the grief, for us the mystery...
And yet thou art not gone
Nor given wholly unto dream and dust:
For, even upon
This lonely western hill of Averoigne
Thy flesh had never visited,
I meet some wise and sentient wraith of thee,
Some undeparting presence, gracious and august.
More luminous for thee the vernal grass,
More magically dark the Druid stone
And in the mind thou art for ever shown
As in a wizard glass;
And from the spirit's page thy runes can never pass.

Song of the Necromancer

OUTLANDERS

To David Warren Ryder

By desert-deepened wells and chasmed ways,
And noon-high passes of the crumbling nome
Where the fell sphinx and martichoras roam;
Over black mountains lit by meteor-blaze,
Through darkness ending not in solar days,
Beauty, the centauress, has brought us home
To shores where chaos climbs in starry foam,
And the white horses of Polaris graze.

We gather, upon those gulfward beaches rolled,
Driftage of worlds not shown by any chart;
And pluck the fabled moly from wild scaurs:
Though these are scorned by human wharf and mart—
And scorned alike the red, primeval gold
For which we fight the griffins in strange wars.

Farewell to Eros

Lord of the many pangs, the single ecstasy!
From all my rose-red temple builded in thy name,
Pass dawnward with no blasphemies of praise or
   blame,
No whine of suppliant or moan of psaltery.

Not now the weary god deserts the worshipper,
The worshipper the god . . . but in some cryptic room
A tocsin tells with arras-deadened tones of doom
That hour which veils the shrine and stills the
   chorister. . .

Others will make libation, chant thy litanies. . .
But, when the glamored moons on inmost Stygia
   glare
And quenchlessly the demon-calling altars flare,
I shall go forth to madder gods and mysteries.

And through Zothique and primal Thule wandering,
A pilgrim to the shrines where elder Shadows dwell,
Perhaps I shall behold such lusters visible
As turn to ash the living opal of thy wing.

Haply those islands where the sunsets sink in rest
Will yield, O Love, the slumber that thou hast not
   given;
Or the broad-bosomed flowers of some vermilion
   heaven
Will make my senses fail as on no mortal breast.

Perchance the fountains of the dolorous rivers four
In Dis, will quench the thirst thy wine assuages never;
And in my veins will mount a twice-infuriate fever
When the black, burning noons upon Cimmeria
   pour.

Song of the Necromancer

Yea, in those ultimate lands that will outlast the Earth,
Being but dream and fable, myth and fantasy,
I shall forget . . . or some image reared of thee,
Dreadful and radiant, far from death, remote from birth.

The Prophet Speaks

City forbanned by seer and god and devil!
In glory less than Tyre or fabled Ys,
But more than they in mere, surpassing evil!

Yea, black Atlantis, fallen beneath dim seas
For sinful lore and rites to demons done,
Bore not the weight of such iniquities!

Your altars with a primal foulness run,
Where the Worm hears the thousand-throated hymn . . .
And all the sunsets write your malison,

And all the stars unrolled from heaven's rim
Declare the doom which I alone may read
In moving ciphers numberless and dim.

O city consecrate to crime and greed!
O scorner of the Muses' messenger!
Within your heart the hidden maggots breed.

Against your piers the nether seas confer;
Against your towers the typhons in their slumber
In sealed abysms darkly mutter and stir.

Clark Ashton Smith

They dream the day when Earth shall disencumber
Her bosom of your sprawled and beetling piles;
When tides that bore your vessels without number

Shall turn your hills to foam-enshrouded isles,
And, ebbing, leave but slime and desolation,
Ruin and rust, through all your riven miles.

On you shall fall a starker devastation
Than came upon Tuloom and Tarshish old,
In you shall dwell the last Abomination.

The dust of all your mansions and the mold
Shall move in changing mounds and clouds disparted
About the wingless air, the footless wold.

The sea, withdrawn from littorals desert-hearted,
Shall leave you to the silence of the sky—
A place fordone, forlorn, unnamed, uncharted,

Where naught molests the sluggish crotali.

Song of the Necromancer

BACCHANTE

Men say the gods have flown;
The Golden Age is but a fading story,
And Greece was transitory:
Yet on this hill hesperian we have known
The ancient madness and the ancient glory.

Under the thyrse upholden,
We have felt the thrilling presence of the god;
And you, Bacchante, shod
With moonfire, and with moonfire all enfolden,
Have danced upon the mystery-haunted sod.

With every autumn blossom,
And with the brown and verdant leaves of vine,
We have filled your hair divine;
From the cupped hollow of your delicious bosom
We have drunk wine, Bacchante, purple wine.

About us now the night
Grows mystical with gleams and shadows cast
By moons for ever past;
And in your steps, O dancer of our delight,
Wild phantoms move, invisible and fast.

Behind, before us sweep
Mænad and Bassarid in spectral rout
With many an unheard shout;
Cithæron looms with every festal steep
Over this hill resolved to dream and doubt.

What Power flows through us,
And makes the old delirium mount amain,
And brims each ardent vein
With passion and with rapture perilous?
Dancer, of whom our votive hearts are fain,

You are that magic urn
Wherefrom is poured the pagan gramarie;
Until, accordingly,
Within our bardic blood and spirit burn
The dreams and fevers of antiquity.

THE PHOENIX

I, I alone have seen the Phoenix fail,
His regal wings their vibrant glories vail
In gyres of baffled crimson, flagging gold,
Below the heaven of his conquests old.
I, I alone have seen the Phœnix build
His pyre with bitter myrrh and spices filled
Amid the ardent waste; and none but I
Has known his death and immortality,
Has watched the yellowy teeth of flame consume
Shell-tinted beak and heaven-painted plume;
Has heard the fatal anguish of his cries
And felt the fierce despair with which he dies
Oblivious of that rebirth to be.
Nor shall another know the mystery
Of flames that turn to plumes, and ashes stirred
To yield once more the fiery-crested bird
With beating rainbow pinions that arise
And take again the lost Sabean skies.

Song of the Necromancer

WITCH-DANCE

As in the Sabbat's ancient round
   With strange and subtle steps you went;
And toward the heavens and toward the ground
   Your steeple-shapen hat was bent
As in the Sabbat's ancient round.

Between the windy, swirling fire
   And all the stillness of the moon,
Sweet witch, you danced at my desire,
   Turning some weird and lovely rune
To paces like the swirling fire.

Your supple youth and loveliness
   A glamor left upon the air:
Whether to curse, whether to bless,
   You wove a stronger magic there
With your lithe youth and loveliness.

Upon the earth your paces wrought
   A circle such as magicians made . . .
And still some hidden thing you sought
   With hands desirous, half afraid,
Beyond the ring your paces wrought.

Your fingers, on the smoke and flame,
   Moved in mysterious conjuring;
You seemed to call a silent Name,
   And lifted like an outstretched wing
Your somber gown against the flame.

What darkling and demonian Lord,
   In fear or triumph, did you call?
Ah! was it then that you implored,
   With secret signs equivocal,
The coming of the covens' Lord?

Sweet witch, you conjured forth my heart
   To answer always at your will!
Like Merlin, in some place apart,
   It lies enthralled and captive still:
Sweet witch, you conjured thus my heart!

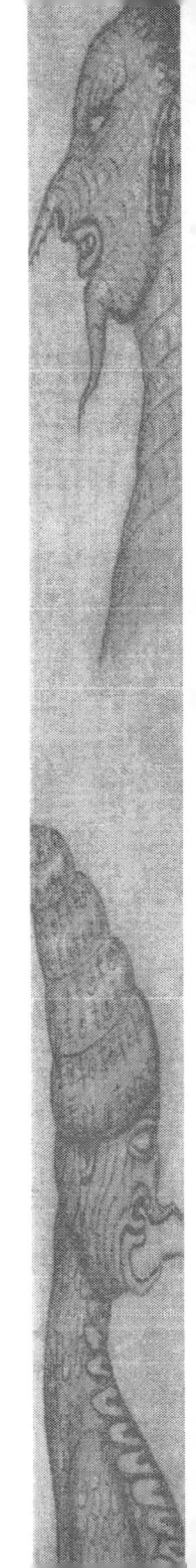

Song of the Necromancer

Necromancy

My heart is made a necromancer's glass,
Where homeless forms and exile phantoms teem,
Where faces of forgotten sorrows gleam,
And dead despairs archaic peer and pass:
Grey longings of some weary heart that was
Possess me, and the multiple, supreme,
Unwildered hope and star-emblazoned dream
Of questing armies. Ancient queen and lass,
Risen vampire-like from out the wormy mould,
Deep in the magic mirror of my heart
Behold their perished beauty, and depart.
And now, from black aphelions far and cold,
Swimming in deathly light on charnel skies,
The enormous ghosts of bygone worlds arise.

Dialogue

One said: "I have seen, from cliffs of doom,
The seven hells flame up in flower
Like a million upas trees that tower,
Massing their realms of poisonous bloom.

I have gone down where dragons writhe,
Mating within the nadir slime;
I have caressed, in some mad clime,
The Gorgon's ringlets, long and lithe."

Another answered: "I have known
The undated hour of agony
When sightless terror leers and crawls

Out of mere soil and simple stone;
When horror seeps from out four walls
And trickles from the unclouded sky."

DESERT DWELLER

There is no room in any town (he said)
To house the towering hugeness of my dream.
It straitens me to sleep in any bed

Whose foot is nearer than the night's extreme.
There is too much of solitude in crowds
For one who has been where constellations teem,

Where boulders meet with boulders, and the clouds
And hills convene; who has talked at evening
With mountains clad in many-colored shrouds.

Men pity me for the scant gold I bring:
Unguessed within my heart the solar glare
On monstrous gems that lit my journeying.

They deem the desert flowerless and bare,
Who have not seen above their heads unfold
The vast, inverted lotus of blue air;

Nor know what Hanging Gardens I behold
With half-shut eyes between the earth and moon
In topless iridescent tiers unrolled.

For them, the planted fields, their veriest boon;
For me, the verdure of inviolate grass
In far mirages vanishing at noon.
For them, the mellowed strings, the strident brass,
The cry of love, the clangor of great horns,
The thunder-burdened ways where thousands pass.

For me, the silence welling from dark urns,
From fountains past the utmost world and sun . . .
To overflow some day the desert bourns . . .

And take the sounding cities one by one.

Song of the Necromancer

THE SORCERER TO HIS LOVE

Within your arms I will forget
The horror that Zimimar brings
Between his vast and vampire wings
From out his frozen oubliette.

The terror born of ultimate space
That gnaws with icy fang and fell,
The sucklings of the hag of hell,
Shall flee the enchantment of your face.

Ah, more than all my wizard art
The circle our delight has drawn:
What evil phantoms thence have gone,
What dreadful presences depart!

Your arms are white, your arms are warm
To hold me from the haunted air,
And you alone are firm and fair
Amid the darkly whirling storm.

Resurrection

Sorceress and sorcerer,
Risen from the sepulcher,
From the deep, unhallowed ground,
We have found and we have bound
Each the other, as before,
With the fatal spells of yore—
With Sabbatic sign, and word
That Thessalian moons have heard.

Sorcerer and sorceress,
Hold we still our heathenness—
Loving without sin or shame—
As in years of stake and flame;
Share we now the witches' madness,
Wake the Hecatean gladness,
Call the demon named Delight
From his lair of burning night.

Love that was, and love to be,
Dwell within this wizardry:
Lay your arm my head beneath
As upon some nighted heath
Where we slumbered all alone
When the Sabbat's rout was flown;
Let me drink your dulcet breath
As in evenings after death.

Witch beloved from of old,
When upon Atlantis rolled
All the dire and wrathful deep,
You had kissed mine eyes asleep;
On my lids shall fall your lips
In the final sun's eclipse;
And your hand shall take my hand
In the last and utmost land.

Song of the Necromancer

TO THE CHIMERA

Unknown chimera, take us, for we tire
Amid the known monotony of things:
Descend, and bearing sunward with bright wings
Our mournful weariness and sad desires,

Pause not to prove the opal shores untrod,
Below thee fading, and the fields of rose;
Till on thy horns of planished silver flows
The sanguine light of Edens lost to God.

There, for the weary sense insatiate,
Primeval sleep from towering scarlet blooms
Would fall in slow and infinite perfumes;

Or we could leave thy crystal wings elate,
Riding the pagan plain with knees that press
The golden flanks of some great centauress.

Do You Forget, Enchantress?

The Muses all are silent for your sake:
While night and distance take
   The hamadryad's hill, the naiad's vale:
   Low droops the hippocentaur's golden tail;
And sleep has whelmed the satyrs in the brake.

Unplucked, the laurels stand as long ago;
The balms of Eros blow
   Rose-red and secret in the cedar's pall . . .
   Do you forget, enchantress, or recall
The world you fashioned once, and now forego?

Where, Venus-like from Lethe and the abyss,
Might rise the abandoned bliss;
   Where the mute Muses bide your summoning word;
   Where darkling faun and daemon drowse unstirred,
Waiting the invocation of your kiss?

Song of the Necromancer

LUNA AETERNALIS

By an alien dream despatched and driven
In a land to strange stars given,
Stars that summoned forth the moon,
Singing a strange red eldritch rune,
I heard the coming of the moon
With tremulous rim that clomb and rang,
Whose rondure on the horizon rang
A gong distinct with silvern clang,
Re-echoing distantly, until,
Arisen soon,
In silent silver stood the moon
Above the horizon ringing still.

Half-waned and hollow was her brow,
And caverned by the night; but now
Her twilight turned the stars' loud rune
To muted music in a swoon,
Her low light lulled the stars to drowse,
Flicker and fail, and vaguely rouse:
I felt the silence come and go
As the red stars muttered low . . .

Old with moonlight lay the night,
And on the desert lay
Ancient and unending light
That assured not of the day;
For the half-moon stood to stay
Fixèd at the heavens' height
And eternal ere the day.
Triumphant stood the moon
In a false and cold and constant noon:
Surely in conflict fell
The true, lost sun of noon;
The golden might of Uriel
Met some white demon of the moon.

Clark Ashton Smith

By an alien dream despatched and driven,
I found a land to demons given,
To silvern, silent demons given
That flew and fluttered from out the moon,
Weaving about her tomb-white face
With mop and mow and mad grimace,
And circling down from the semilune
In a dim and Saturnalian dance,
To pirouette and pause and prance,
To withdraw and advance,
All in a wan eternal dance.

Song of the Neovumancer

"NOT ALTOGETHER SLEEP"

Blithe love, what dubious ponderings bemuse
Thy lover's mind! . . . In me thy memories are
As attar in some alabaster jar . . .
Wholly must I the rose-drawn essence lose
Upon unbalmed oblivion, and diffuse
Its odor on the dust? And shall no star
Of ours illume that ebon calendar
I keep beneath the taproots of the yews?

Or shall, in some ineffable permanence,
The senses merge into one only sense
Holding thine image evermore apart
From suns expired and cycles yet to come—
Where time shall have none other pendulum
Than the remembered pulsings of thy heart?

SONNET FOR THE PSYCHOANALYSTS

When sleep dissolved that super-Freudian dream
where featherless harpies mated while the fed,
I could not find my body: but a thread
of blood on fabled stairs, through mist and steam,
led to a hall of legend. There, in the gleam
of classic lamps, my table-seated head
in gem-bright goblets lazuline and red
saw essences Falernian fall and cream,
self-poured, with cans of seething beer. Beyond,
in balconies that craned on vacant skies,
one booted leg went striding sentry-wise.
It was my own. It guarded with strict care
my heart, a sanguine, ice-girt diamond
imprisoned in some crystal frigidaire.

"O Golden-Tongued Romance"

We found, we knew it dimly
Within a dead life grimly
By guarding time inurned—
A glamor far and olden,
A fulgor night-enfolden,
A flame that in long-darkling Eden burned.

Though hardly then we claimed it,
We yet adored and named it
With a name forgotten now—
A faery word and dawn-like,
A word of gramarie, gone like
An opal bird from off a purple bough . . .

Ah! vain the lamp reluming
The unhaunted vault inhuming
The cold Canopic jar,
And vain the charm recovered
From out the demon-hovered,
Worm-traveled page of pentacled grimoire.

And yet the thing we yearned for,
The thing that we returned for,
From tomb and catacomb,
It may not wholly dwindle
While moon or meteor kindled
A phantom beacon on the ebon foam.

Through ghoul-watched wood unthridden,
By goblin mere and midden,
No ivory horn will blow,
No gold lamp lighten gloom-ward,
But we will carry doom-ward
The broken beauty caught from long ago:

Song of the Necromancer

An echo half evading
The ear, remotely fading
From a far-vibrant lyre,
A long-plucked flower blooming
In the dry urn, a fuming
Myrrh-fragrant ember in a darkened pyre.

Don Quixote on Market Street

Riding on Rosinante where the cars
With dismal unremitting clangors pass,
And people move like curbless energumens
Rowelled by fiends of fury back and forth,
Behold! Quixote comes, in battered mail,
Armgaunt, with eyes of some keen haggard hawk
Far from his eyrie. Gazing right and left,
Over his face a lightning of disdain
Flashes, and limns the hollowness of cheeks
Bronzed by the suns of battle; and his hand
Tightens beneath its gauntlet on the lance
As if some foe had challenged him, or sight
Or unredresséd wrong provoked his ire...

Brave spectre, what chimera shares thy saddle,
Pointing thee to this place? Thy tale is told,
The high, proud legend of all causes lost—
A quenchless torch emblazoning black ages.
Go hence, deluded paladin: there is
No honor here, nor glory, to be won.
Knight of La Mancha, turn thee to the past,
Amid its purple marches ride for aye,
Nor tilt with thunder-driven iron mills
That shall grind on to silence. Chivalry
Has flown to stars unsooted by the fumes
That have befouled these heavens; and romance
Departing, will unfurl her oriflammes
On towers unbuilded in an age to be.
Waste not thy knightliness in wars unworthy,
For time and his alastors shall destroy
Full soon, and bring to stuffless, cloudy ruin
All things that fret thy spirit, riding down
This pass with pandemonian walls, this Hinnom
Where Moloch and where Mammon herd the
   doomed.